How to Draw
Cars and Trucks

This book is dedicated to Justin.

Published in the United States of America by The Child's World®
PO Box 326 • Chanhassen, MN 55317-0326
800-599-READ • www.childsworld.com

Acknowledgments
Design and Production: The Creative Spark, San Juan Capistrano, CA
Series Editor: Elizabeth Sirimarco Budd
Illustration: Rob Court

Library of Congress Cataloging-in-Publication Data
Court, Rob, 1956–
 How to draw cars and trucks / by Rob Court.
    p. cm. — (The Scribbles Institute)
 ISBN 1-59296-148-7 (library bound : alk. paper)
 1. Automobiles in art—Juvenile literature. 2. Trucks in art—Juvenile
literature. 3. Drawing—Technique—Juvenile literature. I. Title.
 NC825.A8C68 2004
 743'.896292—dc22
                                    2004003729

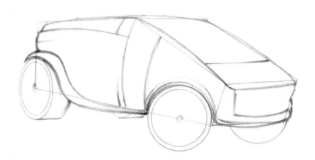

How to Draw
Cars and Trucks

Rob Court

The Child's World®

It is not enough to believe what you see,
you must also understand what you see.

—Leonardo da Vinci

Parents and Teachers,

Children love to draw! It is an essential part of a child's learning process. Drawing skills are used to investigate both natural and constructed environments, record observations, solve problems, and express ideas. The purpose of this book is to help students advance through the challenges of drawing and to encourage the use of drawing in school projects. The reader is also introduced to the elements of visual art—lines, shapes, patterns, form, texture, light, space, and color—and their importance in the fundamentals of drawing.

The Scribbles Institute is devoted to educational materials that keep creativity in our schools and in our children's dreams. Our mission is to empower young creative thinkers with knowledge in visual art while helping to improve their drawing skills. Students, parents, and teachers are invited to visit our Web site—www.scribblesinstitute.com—for useful information and guidance. You can even get advice from a drawing coach!

Contents

Drawing Cars and Trucks

There are many ways to draw cars and trucks. You can draw a race car from your imagination or look at photographs for ideas. You can sketch your family car from memory or while looking at it in the driveway. You can draw using mechanical tools, or you can draw **freehand,** without tools.

The easy steps in this book will help you draw cars and trucks for school projects or for fun. Find a big piece of paper and a pencil. You can get started right now!

Mechanical Tools
A T square helps you make straight, **horizontal** lines. It slides on the edge of your table or drawing board.

Use a triangle with a T square to draw **vertical** and angled lines.

To draw the curved lines for wheels, fenders, and roofs you can use an **ellipse** guide.

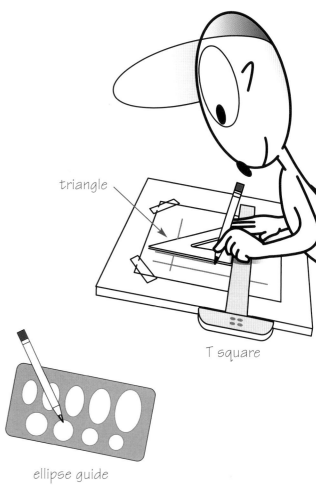

triangle

T square

ellipse guide

Stacked Boxes

Start by stacking two boxes. The bottom box is the vehicle's body. The top box is the cabin. You can position it to the front, middle, or rear of the body. The boxes are guidelines for your drawing.

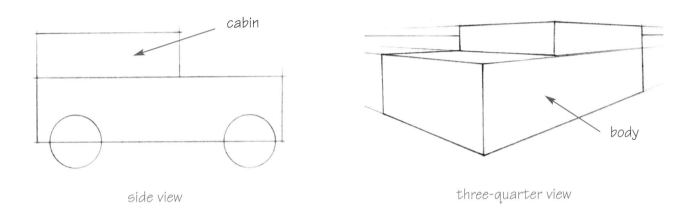

cabin

side view

body

three-quarter view

Guidelines

Lightly sketched guidelines help you to picture your ideas before making a finished drawing. They also help you form the outside edges of your vehicle. **Perspective** guidelines help you to make angled lines in a three-quarter view. Learn more about perspective drawing on page 14.

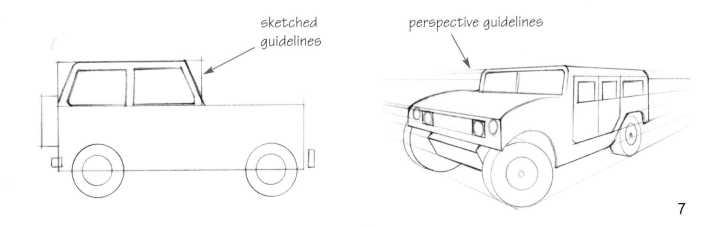

sketched guidelines

perspective guidelines

7

Drawing with Shapes

Drawing a car or truck is easy when you start with basic shapes. Different shapes show the position of its wheels, windows, and bumpers. Sketch these shapes lightly. Then you can erase them later as you finish your picture.

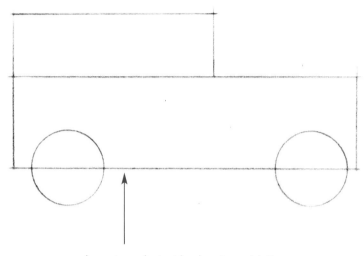

A rectangle is the basic guideline for the body.

"Jeep"
Four-Wheel Drive

1   A Jeep is made to drive on rough terrain. It sits higher off the ground than a car so it can drive over rocks.

Begin by drawing two rectangular boxes for the passenger cabin and the body. Next draw two circles for the tires.

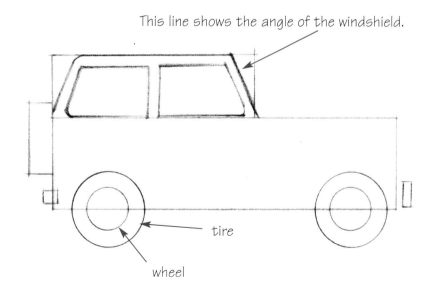

This line shows the angle of the windshield.

tire

wheel

2   Using the rectangles as guidelines, begin lightly sketching the shape of the body. Next, draw smaller circles inside the tires to make the wheels. Rectangular shapes create the spare tire and bumpers. Add the shapes for the windows. Take time to look at the shapes you've drawn. Do you like them?

Drawing with Lines

Drawing an **outline** around the edge of the shapes you've made forms the Jeep's body. Keep drawing until you like the outline. Remember to draw lightly so that you can erase if necessary.

3 Fenders are designed to protect the body from dirt and mud. Leave lots of space between the tires and fenders. Continue by drawing an outline around the shapes of the Jeep.

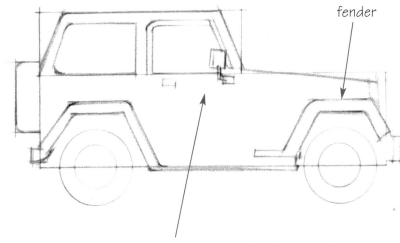

fender

Add details such as the rearview mirror and door handle. Draw smaller, curved lines in areas such as the spare tire and the edges of the body. Adding the details is called tightening your drawing.

lug nut

4 Begin drawing the darker outlines that form the Jeep. Continue adding lines for details such as the door and hood. Draw straight lines to show the reflection of the windows. Draw a pattern of curved lines for the wheels. Don't forget to add the lug nuts.

You can draw many types of vehicles with shapes and lines. Start making a picture of a truck and semitrailer by drawing different rectangles.

Truck and Semitrailer

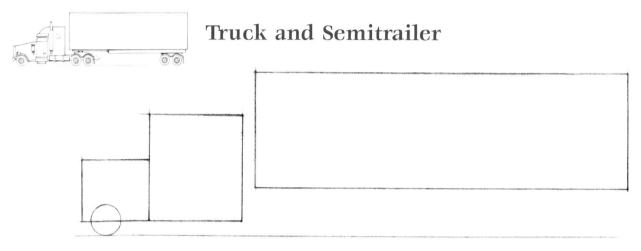

1 Before drawing the tires and wheels of this eighteen-wheeler, draw a horizontal line for the ground. Next, sketch a circle for the front wheel. Then draw rectangle shapes for the truck's body and trailer.

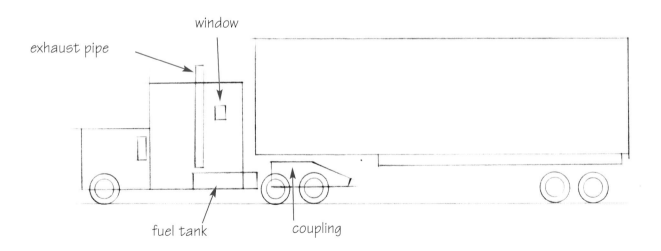

window

exhaust pipe

fuel tank

coupling

2 Draw circles for the tires. You can use a plastic circle template for smooth, curved lines. Sketch smaller circles for the wheels. Next, draw narrow rectangles for the exhaust pipe and fuel tank. A small rectangle makes the window for the sleeping compartment. Lightly sketch angled lines for the coupling that connects the truck and semitrailer.

A T square or ruler comes in handy for making longer guidelines.

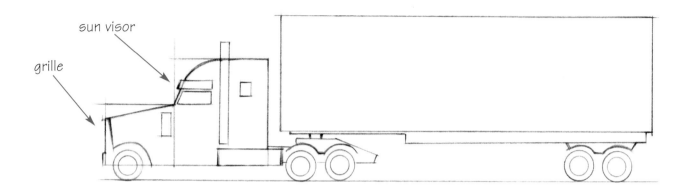

sun visor

grille

3 Take time to sketch the outlines of the truck and semitrailer. Add the windshield, sun visor, grille, and fenders. Notice how the curved and angled outlines are different from the first boxes you drew. You can see the form of the truck's body. Darken the lines for the coupling and fenders.

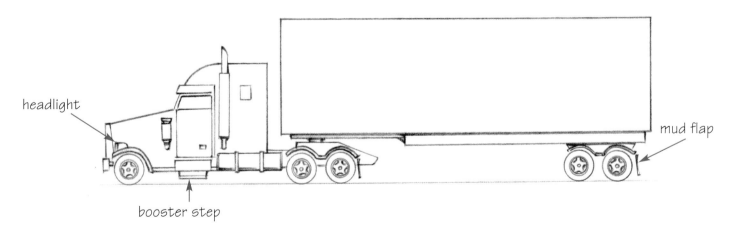

headlight

mud flap

booster step

4 Add details such as the headlights, door handle, booster step, and mud flap. Notice the angled line that makes the top of the exhaust pipe. Using angled and curved lines, carefully draw a darker outline to finish your picture.

Freehand Drawing

Practice freehand drawing by sketching the shapes of a compact car. Then take time to draw accurate outlines and details.

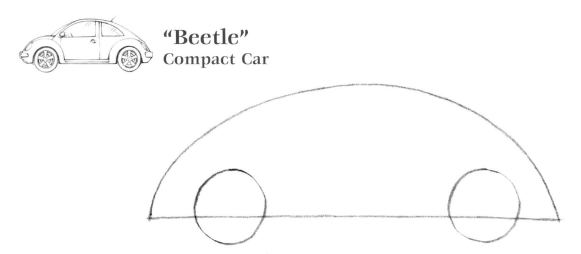

"Beetle"
Compact Car

1 You're drawing the side view of a Beetle. Its body is shaped like an insect, so start by sketching a curved shape instead of boxes. Now make circles that show the position of the tires.

This curved line begins the shape of the front body.

side-view mirror

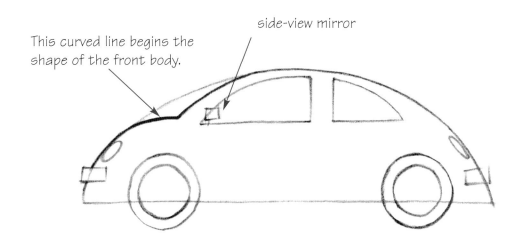

2 Sketch the shapes for the windows. Now sketch ovals for the headlight and taillight. Add the shapes for the front and rear bumpers. Two smaller circles make the wheels. A small rectangle makes the rearview mirror.

Notice how the outlines of the Beetle are different from the first guidelines you drew.

3 Have you seen a Beetle? Try to draw it from memory. Take time to look at the shapes you've drawn. Do you like them? Continue by tightening the outlines around the shapes. Curved and straight lines create the fenders.

4 Using angled and curved lines, carefully draw a darker outline to finish your picture. Add final details like the door handle and bumper.

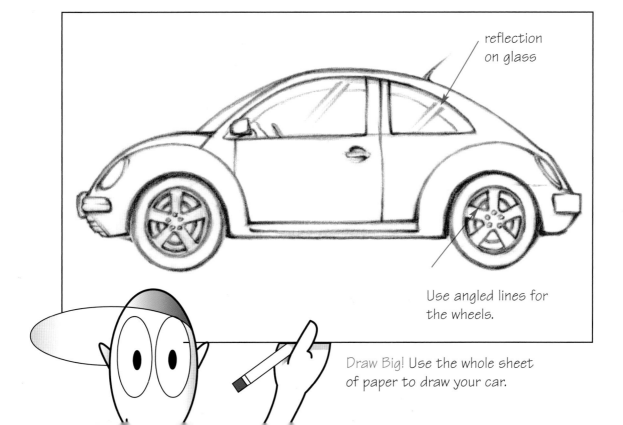

reflection on glass

Use angled lines for the wheels.

Draw Big! Use the whole sheet of paper to draw your car.

Three-Dimensional Form

It's time to make a vehicle look real. With practice, you can change flat shapes into three-dimensional or "3-D" form. Start drawing a military vehicle by making two boxes.

 **"Humvee"** Military Vehicle

1 To draw the Humvee in 3-D, you can use perspective. When an artist uses perspective, some things look close, and other things look far away. Start by drawing the horizon line. This shows where the sky meets the ground. Next, draw a dot at each end of the horizon line. These dots are called vanishing points. Now draw a straight, vertical line just below the center of the horizon line. This is the corner of the Humvee's fender that is nearest to you.

vanishing
point   horizon line   vanishing
                                                                          point

vertical line

2 Lightly draw straight lines from the top of the vertical line to each vanishing point. Next, draw straight lines from the bottom of the vertical line to each vanishing point. You can use a ruler to draw these guidelines. To complete the box, make vertical lines to place the two corners that are farther away.

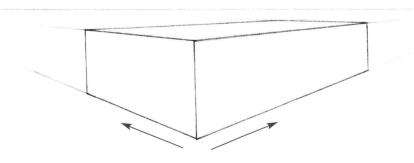

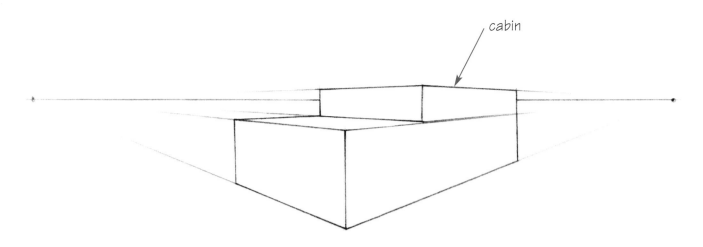
cabin

3 Now draw the box for the cabin. Start with the corner of the cabin closest to you, then draw the guidelines that connect to each vanishing point. Think of the basic form of the Humvee as a smaller box stacked on top of a larger one.

HOT TIP ### Check Guidelines

With a ruler, check each guideline to be sure it is drawn at a direct angle to the vanishing point. Remember to draw light guidelines so that you can erase them later.

4 Sketch an oval for the front tire. Draw guidelines from the top and bottom of the tire to the vanishing point at right. Now draw the rear tire to fit between the top and bottom guidelines. Make sure all guidelines are drawn to the vanishing point on the right side of your paper.

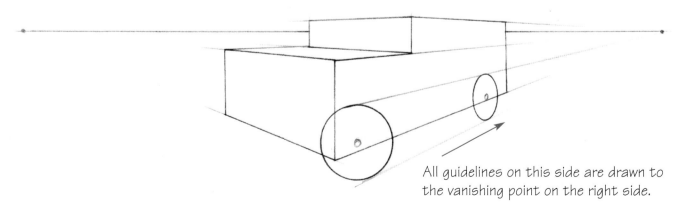

All guidelines on this side are drawn to the vanishing point on the right side.

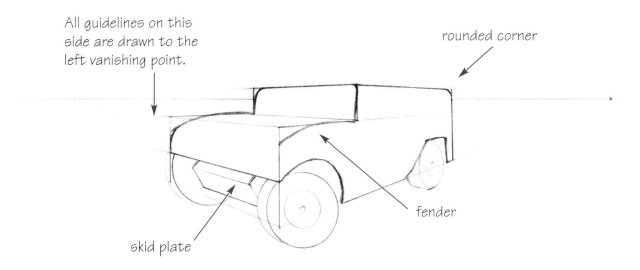

All guidelines on this side are drawn to the left vanishing point.

rounded corner

skid plate

fender

5 Continue by sketching outlines around the box shapes. Draw the curved lines that make the fenders. The tires are positioned under the fenders. Add curved lines for the outside edges of the tires. Draw ovals for the wheels, centered inside the tires. Draw angled lines for the skid plate.

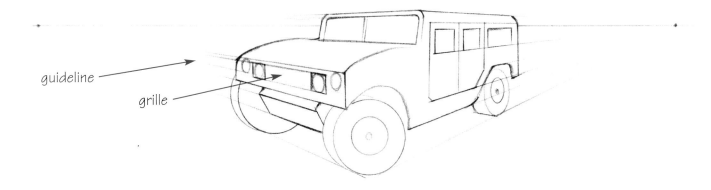

guideline

grille

6 Here's where guidelines are very helpful. Notice in the drawing above how the top and bottom of the headlights are positioned between guidelines. The grille is also positioned between these guidelines. Draw guidelines before sketching the windshield, side windows, and doors.

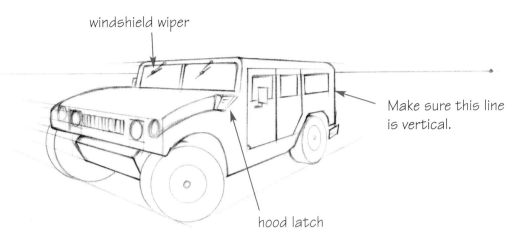

windshield wiper

Make sure this line is vertical.

hood latch

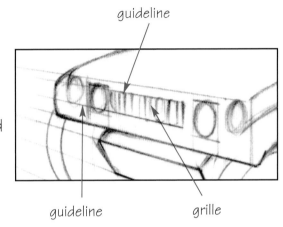

guideline

guideline

grille

7 Taking time to make corrections will make your Humvee look more realistic. Continue sketching the outlines that form the Humvee. Add details for the grille, windshield wipers, side-view mirror, and hood latch. Keep sketching until the angles of perspective are correct.

8 It's time to finish your picture by drawing the final outlines. Carefully draw the treads of the large, off-road tires. Add final details such as door handles, hood vents, and heavy-duty wheels.

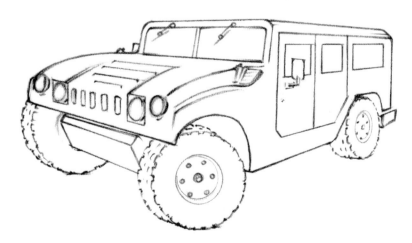

Congratulations! By completing your perspective drawing, you have joined the ranks of Renaissance artists such as Albrecht Dürer and Leonardo da Vinci. These masters helped to invent perspective drawing.

Light and Shadows

Tones are lighter and darker shades of a color. By using tones, you can create shadows. Drawing shadows helps you see the form of a dragster and the ground underneath it.

Dragster

1 A dragster is different from other cars. Its engine is larger. It has huge rear tires for extra traction. Start by sketching the basic box shapes for the car's body and cockpit.

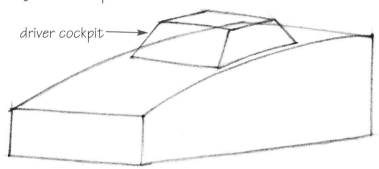

driver cockpit

2 Sketch the shapes for the headlights and grille. Sketch the curved lines for the position of the front and rear fenders. Sketch the shapes for stabilizing fins, exhaust pipes, and the air intake.

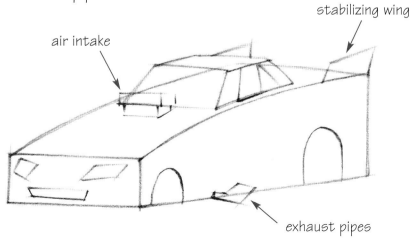

stabilizing wing

air intake

exhaust pipes

Light Source

Places where light comes from are called light sources. The sun is a light source. A lamp is also a light source. In the drawing below, a light source shines on a sphere. How do the shadows change as the light changes position?

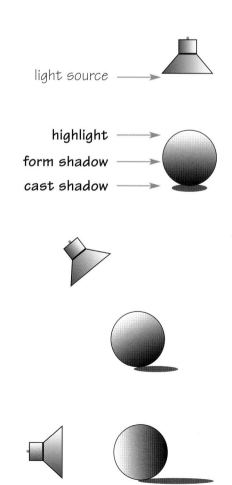

light source

highlight
form shadow
cast shadow

18

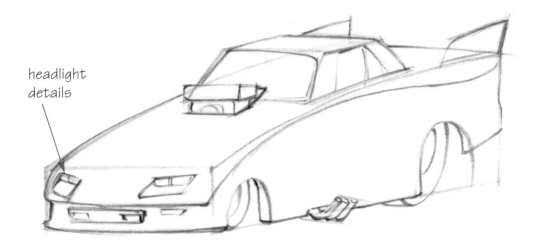

headlight
details

3 Before adding shadows, draw the outlines that form the dragster's body. The body is
   low to the ground in the front, and high off the ground in back. This makes it difficult
to see the tires and wheels. Keep sketching outlines for the headlights, air intake, exhaust
pipes, and windows. Erase all guidelines before shading.

4 Finish drawing features such as the engine and headlights. Start drawing the shadows
   where there is no light coming from the light source. Hold your pencil on its side, press
firmly, and begin drawing the darkest shadows. Shadows will be lighter where more light
shines. Lighten the pressure on your pencil as you draw lighter shadows. Fade the shadows
into the white of the paper. The highlighted areas do not have shading.

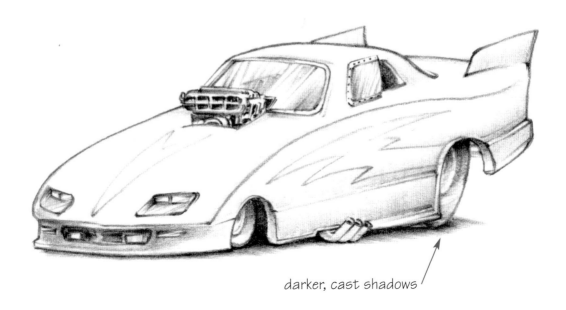

darker, cast shadows

Drawing Ideas

Drawing helps you share ideas with other people. Taking time to make a sketch lets others see your concept of a futuristic sport utility vehicle (SUV). Practice sketching quickly. Make changes to your picture as you think of new ideas.

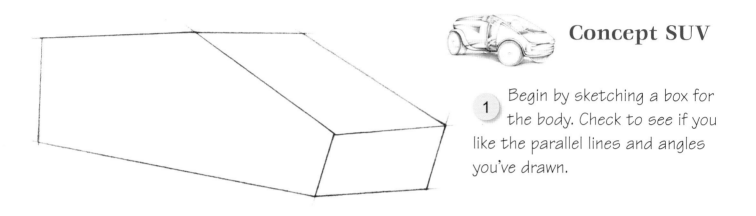

Concept SUV

1 Begin by sketching a box for the body. Check to see if you like the parallel lines and angles you've drawn.

2 Next, begin sketching lines for the windshield and placement of the front grille. Two quick, curved lines mark the position of the door. Draw two ovals for the front and rear tires. Add two smaller ovals for the center of the wheels.

The corner of the box meets the center of the wheel.

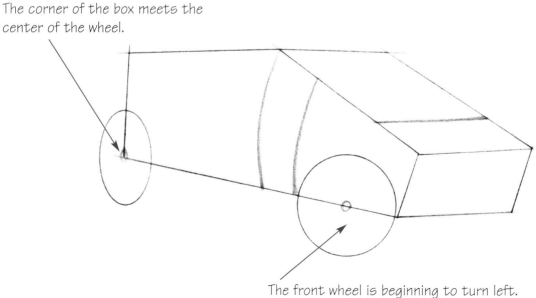

The front wheel is beginning to turn left.

This curved guideline shows the top edge of the SUV's glass body.

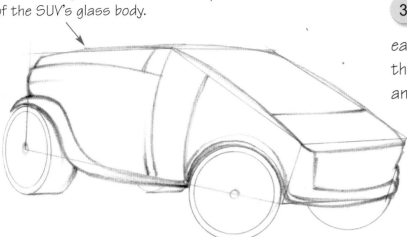

3 The body's design has many curved lines that flow into each other. Continue by sketching the outlines of its glass top, door, and windshield. Add curved lines for the fenders and tires.

Concept Artist

Before a car is built, a concept artist draws a plan of what it will look like. This helps manufacturers design useful cars for the future. Concept artists also help movie directors design futuristic vehicles for movies before filming begins.

Your Own Style

Everyone has their own personal style of handwriting. Concept artists develop their personal styles of drawing, too. Some use loose, bold pencil strokes for final drawings. Others use sharper lines to show important details. Think about a style that's comfortable for you to use when drawing.

4 Finish your picture by shading with different gray tones. Use a gray tone for areas of glass. Use a darker tone to show shadows behind the seats, between fenders and tires, and on the ground.

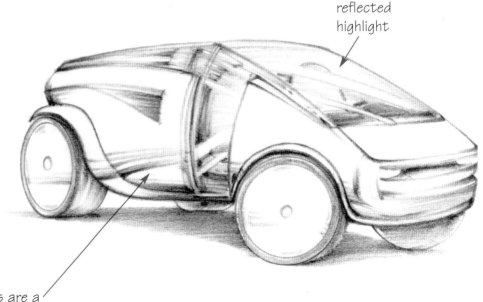

reflected highlight

These lines are a reflection of the ground.

Patterns

You can create patterns in your drawing by repeating lines or shapes. Add a wood-grain pattern to a picture of a classic car.

"Woody"
Station Wagon

1 The Woody was popular with surfers in the 1960s. They used it for carrying their long, heavy surfboards. It got its nickname because its doors are covered with panels of wood. Start by sketching two boxes. Check the angles of your guidelines.

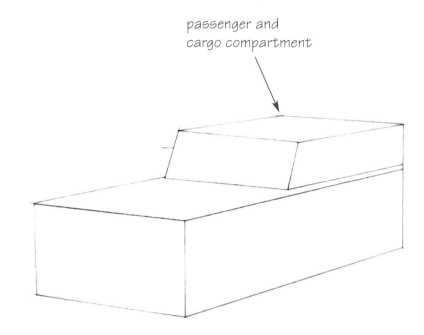

passenger and cargo compartment

2 Use the guidelines to help you draw the shape of the Woody's body. Sketch the shapes for the windows, headlights, and turn signals. Add a rectangle for the grille.

Use curved lines to draw the hood and fenders. Lines that show roundness are called contour lines.

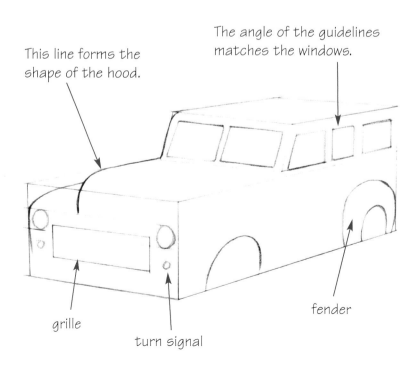

This line forms the shape of the hood.

The angle of the guidelines matches the windows.

grille

turn signal

fender

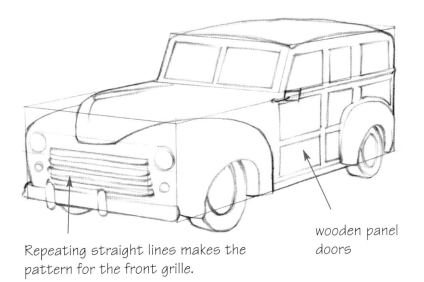

Repeating straight lines makes the pattern for the front grille.

wooden panel doors

3 Sketch the shapes for the tires and wheels. Begin sketching the outlines that form the body. Carefully draw contour lines that form the fenders and hood. Draw an outline to show the edges of the canvas roof. Add the panel doors, front bumper, and grille.

4 To finish your picture, draw the darker, final outlines. Finish the front bumper and add windshield wipers. Use a dark tone to fill in the pattern of the grille. Add a gray tone to the tires. Also include the shadow that is cast by the fenders onto the tires. Carefully draw the wood patterns on the panel doors.

Since this Woody is over 50 years old, it is called a classic car. Draw an old-style surfboard in the rear cargo area.

Shading shows the texture of the canvas roof.

23

Space and Composition

The white space on your paper can be transformed into a place to park a convertible. The way you divide the space is called composition. Begin your composition by drawing the horizon line. This shows where the ground meets the sky. Draw the line to the edges of your paper.

Classic Convertible

horizon line

1 Start by drawing a box for the car's body. Check the angles of your guidelines.

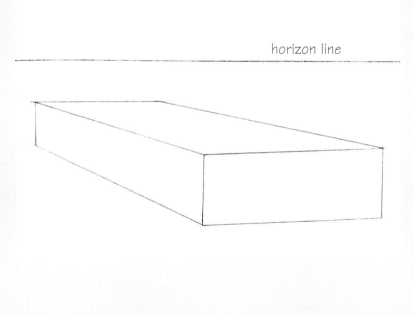

Parallel Lines

Before moving to step 2, take a moment to look at the box you've drawn. Make sure the angles of the parallel lines are the same, as shown above. Parallel lines point in the same direction but never touch.

2 Draw the shape for the windshield. Next, sketch curved lines for the wheel wells. Draw guidelines to help you place the headlights and front grille.

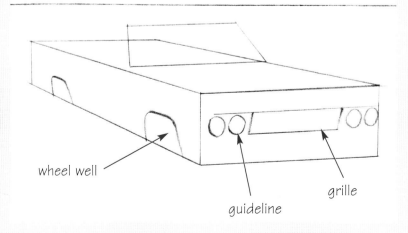

wheel well

guideline

grille

3 Next, sketch the front bumper. Its lines are parallel to the guidelines of the grille. Draw a narrow rectangle for the rearview mirror. Add lines around the edge of the area where the passengers sit. Lightly sketch the ovals for the tires. Sketch them a few times to get the angle you want. An ellipse guide helps you to draw sharp lines.

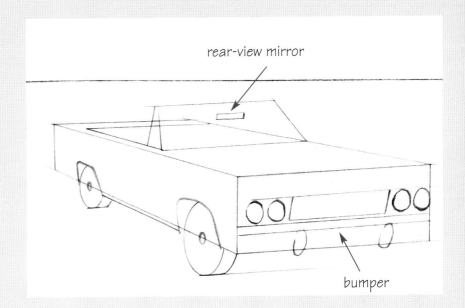

rear-view mirror

bumper

4 Take time to sketch the outlines that form the convertible's body. Tighten your lines until you like what you've drawn. Begin adding other elements to your composition.

By drawing the mountains on the horizon line, they look farther away than the trees.

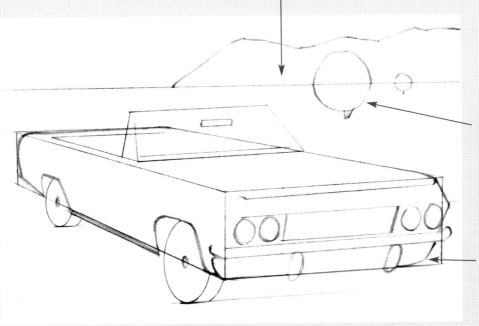

By drawing this tree larger, it looks closer than the smaller tree. It is drawn in the space behind the car. The trees are in the background, and the car is in the foreground.

The corners of the car's body are curved inside of the box-shaped guidelines.

The front tire is closer to you than the rear tire. To show this in your drawing, make the front tire bigger.

5 Continue with darker outlines around the car's body and details such as the headlights, steering wheel, and seats. Add ovals for the wheels.

Draw the contour lines for the edges of the trees. They are in the distance, so you don't need to draw the individual leaves.

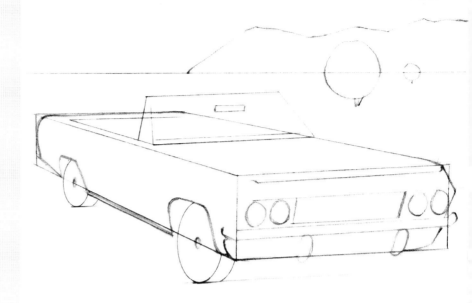

6 Finish your picture by carefully drawing darker contour lines. Add gray tones for shadows on the convertible's body and tires. By repeating lines, you can create the patterns for the seats and the grille. Add a light gray tone to the mountains. Shade the side of the trees that are turned away from the sun. Don't forget to draw the shadows that are cast on the ground.

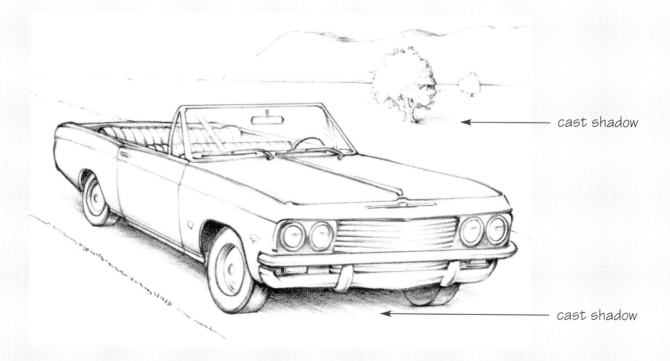

cast shadow

cast shadow

Which Pencil Should You Use?

A standard "2B" or "2SOFT'" pencil works well for most drawings, but other pencils can make your drawing even more interesting.

Pencils are numbered according to how hard or soft the lead is. You'll find this number written on the pencil. A number combined with the letter "H" means the lead is hard (2H, 3H, 4H, etc.). When you draw with hard leads, the larger the number you use, the lighter and thinner your lines will be.

A number combined with the letter "B" means the lead is soft (2B, 4B, 6B, etc.). The lines you draw will get darker and thicker with larger numbers. Sometimes you will read "2SOFT" or "2B" on standard pencils used for school-work. When you see the letter "F" on a pencil, it means the pencil is of medium hardness.

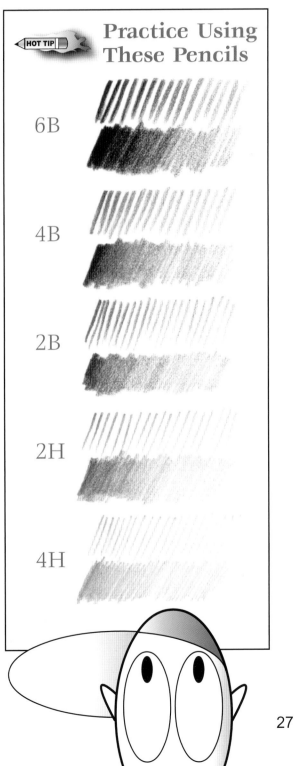

HOT TIP

Practice Using These Pencils

6B

4B

2B

2H

4H

27

Drawing with Color

By using colored pencils, you can make the picture of a race car more exciting. Create the colors of its specially designed body by mixing yellow, blue, red, and black.

 **Race Car**

1 A race car sits low to the ground so it can turn corners at high speeds. The lines of the race car's body are angled so the wind will glide right over it. Sketch the boxes shown below. Draw the angled lines that make the windshield. Notice the angles of the lines for the rear fender and airfoil.

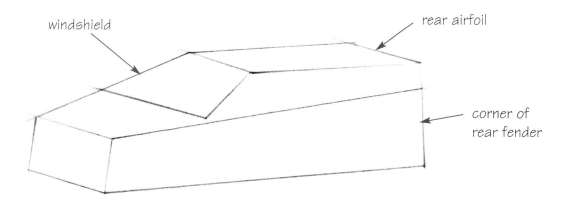

windshield

rear airfoil

corner of rear fender

2 Use the boxes as guidelines to begin sketching the outlines of the race car. Compare the lines that you've drawn with the picture shown below. Do the angles of the windshield and cockpit look the same in your drawing? Does the outline for the front of the body look the same? Continue by adding the side window and circles for the tires.

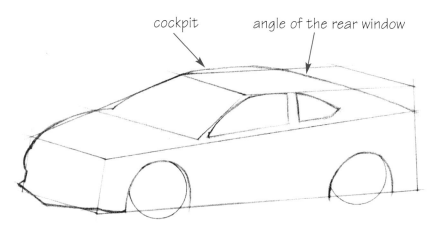

cockpit

angle of the rear window

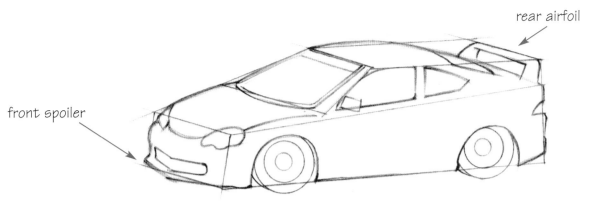

rear airfoil

front spoiler

③ Carefully draw outlines for the cockpit, headlights, side-view mirror, and airfoil. Add two circles for the wheels. When you like the lines you've drawn, carefully erase all guidelines and prepare to add color.

Create a design on the side of the car and add a racing number.

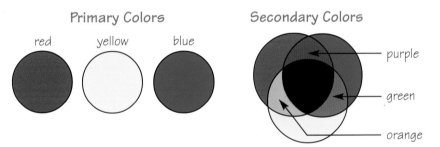

Primary Colors

red   yellow   blue

Secondary Colors

purple

green

orange

HOT TIP

Mixing primary colors creates secondary colors.

Adding one color on top of another while drawing is called layering. To learn how to layer primary colors, try using only yellow, blue, red, and black in this drawing.

④ Lightly shade the race car's body with a yellow pencil. From what direction is the light shining? Apply more pressure to darken areas where there are shadows.

The yellow is darker on this side of the car because there is less light.

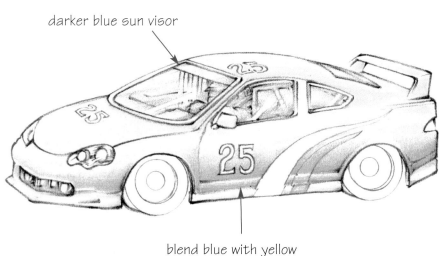

darker blue sun visor

blend blue with yellow

5 Next, add blue to your drawing. Shade the windshield and side windows with a light blue tone. Add a darker tone of blue for the sun visor and the design on the body.

Shade the bottom edge of the car with blue. Fade it into the yellow as shown at left. What color do you get when you mix blue with yellow?

Mixing Colored Pencils Is Fun!

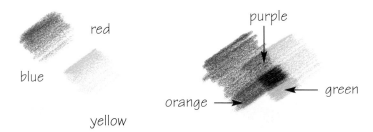

red

blue

yellow

purple

orange

green

6 Add a layer of light red to make an orange rear airfoil. A darker red tone brings attention to the design on the side of the car. What color do you get when you add red over blue? Shading with black creates the 3-D form of the race car. Highlights and shadows create realistic details.

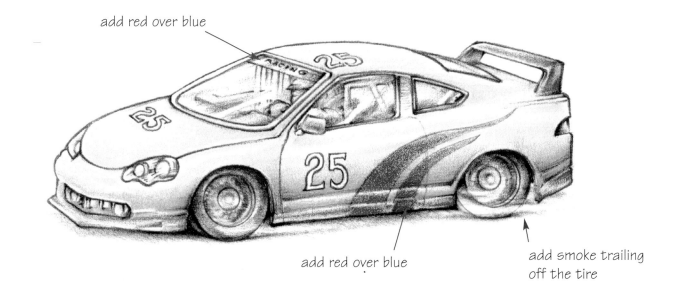

add red over blue

add red over blue

add smoke trailing off the tire

The Artist's Studio

Artists need a special place where they can relax and concentrate on their work.

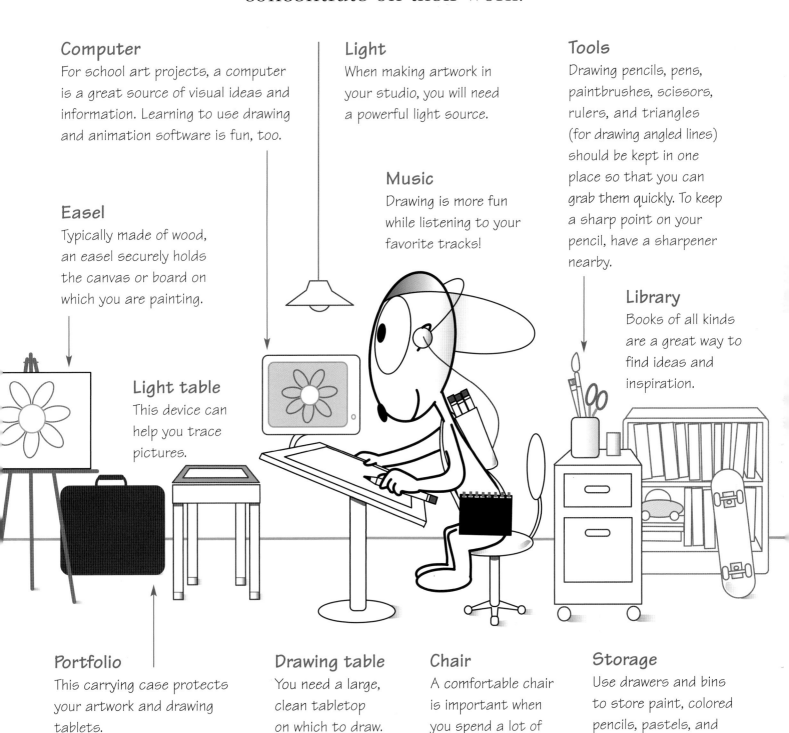

Computer
For school art projects, a computer is a great source of visual ideas and information. Learning to use drawing and animation software is fun, too.

Easel
Typically made of wood, an easel securely holds the canvas or board on which you are painting.

Light table
This device can help you trace pictures.

Light
When making artwork in your studio, you will need a powerful light source.

Music
Drawing is more fun while listening to your favorite tracks!

Tools
Drawing pencils, pens, paintbrushes, scissors, rulers, and triangles (for drawing angled lines) should be kept in one place so that you can grab them quickly. To keep a sharp point on your pencil, have a sharpener nearby.

Library
Books of all kinds are a great way to find ideas and inspiration.

Portfolio
This carrying case protects your artwork and drawing tablets.

Drawing table
You need a large, clean tabletop on which to draw.

Chair
A comfortable chair is important when you spend a lot of time drawing.

Storage
Use drawers and bins to store paint, colored pencils, pastels, and other supplies.

Glossary

A **cast shadow** is the shadow that a person, animal, or object throws on the ground, a wall, or other feature.

An **ellipse** is a narrow oval shape.

A **form shadow** is a shadow in a drawing that shows the form or shape of a person, animal, or object.

Freehand drawing is drawing without tools such as T squares, rulers, or triangles.

A **highlight** is the area or areas in a drawing that receive the most light from the light source.

A **horizontal** line moves from side to side; a person lying down is in a horizontal position.

An **outline** is a line that shows the shape of an object, animal, or person.

Perspective is the art of picturing objects on a flat surface, like a piece of paper, so that they appear to be in the distance.

A **vertical** line is drawn straight up and down; a person standing up is in a vertical position.

Index

About the Author

Rob Court is a designer and illustrator. He started the Scribbles Institute™ to help people learn about the importance of drawing and visual art.